What She Said
Ilisha Thiru Purcell

VERVE
POETRY PRESS
BIRMINGHAM

PUBLISHED BY VERVE POETRY PRESS
https://vervepoetrypress.com
mail@vervepoetrypress.com

All rights reserved
© 2025 Ilisha Thiru Purcell
The right of Ilisha Thiru Purcell to be identified as author of this work has been asserted in accordance with section 77 of the Copyright, Designs and Patents Act 1988.

No part of this work may be reproduced, stored or transmitted in any form or by any means, graphic, electronic, recorded or mechanical, without the prior written permission of the publisher.

FIRST PUBLISHED APRIL 2025

Printed and bound in the UK
by Imprint Digital, Exeter

ISBN: 978-1-913917-63-0

In my endeavour to be human
I wish to leave the flowers in the trees
　—Sivaramani

The following sequence of poems was inspired by classical Tamil love poetry, *akam* poetry. In this classical form, distinctive external landscapes mirror internal experiences and states of nameless personae.

I have followed the classical conventions, with the Tamil poetics transposed to the landscape of the North East of England where I grew up and currently live.

Inspired by the classical landscapes, I have created five distinctive landscapes and utilised the form to explore sexual violence, sexuality, and climate change.

More information on these landscapes can be found on page 40.

The number preceding each poem relates to the order they were written in.

What She Said

22. What Her Friend Said

We danced like minnows
flitting out of the water
bodies weightless, breathless.

Around us men believed they were herons
their mouths glinting bills
their unblinking eyes taking stock.

44. What She Said

Before becoming after
is the hush of the hand
felling a tree, the din of fingers
that later pluck
the splutters of growth.

25. What She Said

The heat cracks my vision,
everywhere I see crows wielding his tongue.

I seek the river I waded in as a child
hoping for blue-fresh water.

But my eyes only meet
the fissured face
of what was once its bed.

49. What She Said

Wildfire ash becomes skin
he has not touched,
air so dry it snaps in my throat.

All around there are limbs of trees
broken, pointing at the shards
for me to mourn.

10. What the Women Said

Like the freshwater salmon
boiled in its own home
where do we have that is safe?
Are they to grow lungs
and we to live up in the clouds?

There is no end to the taking of land,
there is no end to the taking of bodies
of water.

14. What She Said to the Trees

There were no passersby.
Only you saw the thief and what he took.

You who have been sapped of your speech
and wither as if ageing backwards.

I have my voice
but they look at me
as if I speak the language of leaves.

They turn from me and my browning tongue
as they turn from the truth of your withering.

34. What She Said

Check
that the sun has kept its promise

wait for the sky to flicker
grey and blue
smell the trees
attending their own cremation
hear the silence
as bees pause mid-air

check
that you are ready to run.

37. What Her Friend Said to Her

In your eyes
I see the same hare that lives
in my heart.

I too know how it freezes
I too know the patter
of its nails against grey stone,
that scratch of desperation.

38. What She Said

The darkness looms

mountains you have to scramble down
on your hands and knees.

Wisps of your skin
held by sun-yellow gorse.

The air thick with coconut
flesh.

42. What She Said to the Roe Deer

I only saw you for a moment,
that flash of white.

I wonder if others saw it
as flesh yet to be claimed,
the centre of a target.

Our eyes met and as you ran
your white and brown fur blended
like my own skin.

40. What Hadrian's Wall Said to Her

Become a ball of fissured edges.
Slot yourself within me
you'll harden into history,
either hand dipped in the sea
head always facing the sky.

You're stone now
You're stone now.

39. What She Said to Silvas Capitalis*

In the forest stands a head
its mouth and eyes an opening.

Hollow me out like this
piece me together with no skin, no bones.

Make me entirely out of larch,
let my nerves be pine.

---

* A sculpture in Kielder Forest by the American artist collective SIMPARCH.

41. What The Lady of the North Said*

There is always a witness –
the trees whisper
and the clouds never turn away.

Even if you think you're alone
rebellion as fragile
as a dandelion seed,
just wait

the wind will be at your back
the waves will caress your bones.

---

* Rock and soil sculpture of a woman reclining designed by Charles Jencks. Also known as Northumberlandia.

47. What She Said

Out of my window
the sky curdles into night,
it is too much to hear the men's
laughter bouncing off the brick.

I let the seagulls' cry
carry me away.

33. What She Said

Sleep, unlike the rain, does not come.

Though even there I cannot escape your face,
it is the housefly in my ear bringing me back.

If I could, I would squish the memory of it
watch the blood drain, stain
my hands and the wall
rather than my night.

21. What Her Friend Said

It is only when the world is sleeping
that you will speak of it.
Your words budding
like henbit forced to bloom.

Soon, pink-purple petals will surround us
and as I reach to pick one out of your hair
you'll flinch.

9. What She Said

From my window I watch
a robin hold a wish-bone of twig
in the clamp of its beak.

I nestle in the sight,
nicking my cheek as I brood
into the past.

In the morning the nest is destroyed
by a swift fist.

50. What She Said

Yesterday, out of blood and ink I grew orchids on my ribcage.

A whole landscape he has not touched.

32. What She Said

What will be on this path before me?
A grimace of a cliff face?
Seagulls with their peace-breaking caws?
Glass beneath the sand?
Litter in the spume of the sea?

Tell me, and I hope you do not know.

27. What Her Mother Said

On the shore I unravel
the secrets that live under my skin.

Shame is pleated around me like a sari
that belonged to my mother,
her mother and the mother of her.

I place the frayed silk into the sea
pray I do not turn back as I walk away.

28. What She Said

I write the truth that they will not listen to
on the sand, look –
how it's washed away.

The truth now lives in the sea
swimming alongside dolphins
resting against a flash of coral.

It is happy there
it seems it has no place on dry land.

16. What Her Father Said

I've come to Shields to buy fish

but with their glassy eyes level with mine
fins slicked with iced-fear
I can only whisper an apology.

I will return home empty-handed
and no one will notice,
their eyes busy watching
what the day will reel in.

36. What She Said

I stand before Marsden Rock and try to skim stones.

At first they
fall
coins into a fountain,
a wish left ungranted.

Finally, a stone skims
pirouetting
once, twice, thrice on the water
and for those three leaps I hold my breath

I forget
and I am the stone bounding,
light as a hopeful thought.

When the stone plummets
I remember it all again.

26. What She Said

This strip of blue amid green
the dene parting its legs in bloom.

I grip this moment
but the image of the forest razed
water syphoned
the legs of the earth held open
flits before my eyes.

I listen to the song of the water
falling
birds writing poems in the air –

it all sounds like a page trying to turn.

1. What She Said

I will tell no one else
how I   you,
the way one drop of dew
slides down the fold of a leaf.

2. What He Said

Within me is a lake
that only you and I know the directions of.
Water as clear as your iris,
as calm as your hand resting on mine.

The lake embraces the sky
as I hold you in my arms.

8. What She Said to Him

Meet me under the Shoe Tree*
the scent of wild garlic sewing us together.

What is our need for stars
under shoes who've found their match?
Who spend each day aware
of time's thin branch
and still swing to the beat of the forest.

Let's name a pair after us,
walk off into the night
as they dance in the sky.

---

* The Shoe Tree is a tree in Newcastle where people have thrown pairs of shoes to hang from its branches.

11. What She Said to Her Lover at the Great North Road

For a moment there is no traffic.
The daffodils lift their heads
and drink the dregs of fumes,
cups full of the sun's embrace.

But what could compare to you
turning to face me
illuminated by my love?

13. What She Said to Him

We fell to the floor
and the carpet became grass
shimmering with dew.

It was too early for stars
but your touch
became a constellation point
that only we knew the name of,

my body celestial.

6. What She Said to Him

Touch me
the way the sunset kisses the moor
daily, differently each time.

Yesterday it was a caress
an exhale of pink

today, no inch of sky untouched
as red gathers into orange
like crumpled sheets.

30. What She Said to Him

The curves of my body wax and wane,
a blossom moon after we—

but what word is there for what we have shared?

There is just the flash of the full moon
behind caresses of clouds,
the reflection cradled
in the puddle on our doorstep

a drop of the celestial.

THE FIVE LANDSCAPES*

Stage	Assault and immediate aftermath	Hypervigilance, flashbacks, fear
Landscape	1: Climate devastation - wildfires, flash floods, storms	2: Expansive hills, rocks, and mountains
Season	Out of season	Summer
Time	Any	Midday
Flower	-	Heather, gorse, waxcap, melancholy thistle, yellow rattle, wood cranesbill, sundew
Animal	-	Rabbit, hare, barn owl, roe deer, adder, bumblebee
Trees	Felled, burnt	Aspen, common juniper, sycamore
Water	Flood, drought	Peat bog
Location	-	Northumberland National Park Hadrian's Wall Northumberlandia

Isolation, numbness, nightmares	Healing begins	Love and sexuality
3: Domestic sphere	4: Coast	5: Forests and fields
Autumn	Winter	Spring
Night	Dawn/ dusk	Mainly daytime/ sunset
Henbit, deadnettle, couch grass, ragwort	Seaweed, spring squill, sea bindweed	Daffodil, cow parsley, wild garlic, windflower, rhododendron
Seagull, robin, spider, woodlouse, housefly, ant, domestic cat, domestic dog	Dolphin, puffin, kittiwake, cormorant, razorbill, sea swallow, grey seal	Starling, swan, cow, finch, nuthatch, magpie
Sessile oak, European ash, horse chestnut	-	Holly, cypress, redwood, cherry blossom
Rain, cloud	Sea	Waterfall, lake
-	Whitley Bay Tynemouth Marsden Rock	Jesmond Dene Town Moor Heaton Park Durham Riverside Exhibition Park

ON THE FIVE LANDSCAPES

* The headings in this table were based on A. K. Ramanujan's "Some Features of the Five Landscapes" (Ramanujan, 1967, pp.92) and adapted for the location and themes of this sequence.

Ramanujan, A. K. (1967) *The Interior Landscape,* New York: New York Review of Books.

ABOUT THE AUTHOR

Ilisha Thiru Purcell is an award-winning Sri Lankan-Scottish poet from Newcastle upon Tyne. She was part of the inaugural Poets of Colour Incubator Programme and was a Young Creative Associate with New Writing North. Ilisha was a Poet in Residence at the 2025 StAnza Poetry Festival, winning the Futurist Award. She has been shortlisted for the James Berry Prize and Nine Arches' Primers. Her work has appeared in publications such as *Bi+ Lines Anthology, Butcher's Dog*, and *Third Space Anthology*. @ilishadoespoetry

ACKNOWLEDGEMENTS

These poems mean so much to me – thank you to everyone who understands just how much.

I got the inspiration for the sequence while reading A. K. Ramanujan's *The Interior Landscape*. I am incredibly grateful for his translations of classical Tamil love poetry.

Shash, thank you for your support, guidance, and belief. This process wouldn't have been the same without you.

Thank you to New Writing North and North of Tyne Combined Authority for supporting my early ideas for this work.

To Written Off Publishing and Nine Arches Press who published two of the poems in this sequence.

To Stuart at VERVE for giving these poems a home.

To Rebecca, thank you for helping me to create the poetry film that accompanies this sequence and us becoming friends along the way.

To my parents for their unwavering love.

To Izzy, Olivia, and Mymona.

And to Eamon, I love you. All the poems in the final section are for you.

ABOUT VERVE POETRY PRESS

Verve Poetry Press is an award-winning press which focussed initially on meeting a local need in Birmingham - a need for the vibrant poetry scene here in Brum to find a way to present itself to the poetry world via publication. Co-founded by Stuart Bartholomew and Amerah Saleh, it now publishes poets from all corners of the UK and beyond - poets that speak to the city's varied and energetic qualities and will contribute to its many poetic stories.

Added to this is a colourful pamphlet series, many featuring poets who have performed at our sister festival - and a poetry show series which captures the magic of longer poetry performance pieces by festival alumni such as Polarbear, Suhaiymah Manzour-Khan and Imogen Stirling.

The press has been voted Most Innovative Publisher at the Saboteur Awards, and has won the Publisher's Award for Poetry Pamphlets at the Michael Marks Awards.

Like the festival, we strive to think about poetry in inclusive ways and embrace the multiplicity of approaches towards this glorious art.

https://vervepoetrypress.com
@VervePoetryPres
mail@vervepoetrypress.com